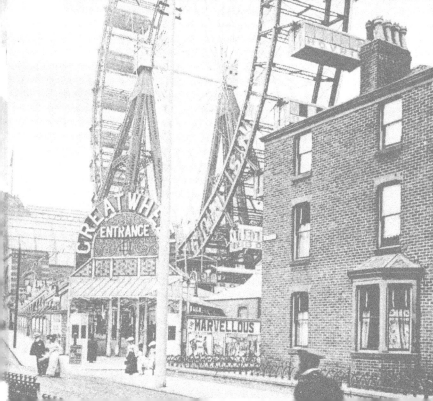

BLACKPOOL

HISTORY TOUR

First published 2015

Amberley Publishing
The Hill, Stroud,
Gloucestershire, GL5 4EP
www.amberley-books.com

Copyright © Allan W. Wood and
Ted Lightbown, 2015

The right of Allan W. Wood and Ted
Lightbown to be identified as the
Authors of this work has been asserted
in accordance with the Copyrights,
Designs and Patents Act 1988.

ISBN   978 1 4456 4623 7 (print)
ISBN   978 1 4456 4624 4 (ebook)

British Library Cataloguing in
Publication Data.
A catalogue record for this book is
available from the British Library.

Typesetting by Amberley Publishing.
Printed in Great Britain.

INTRODUCTION

It could be said that there can be no history without change, and this is certainly true in the case of a visual history of Blackpool. The town, whose motto is 'Progress', has changed a great deal since, as a coastal hamlet, it first began to attract visitors from the middle of the eighteenth century. It has grown since those times to become the UK's premier holiday resort and this is primarily due to the 7 miles of wide sandy 'golden' beach, the often bracing west-facing sea frontage, the proximity of Blackpool to the industrial towns and people of the North of England and Blackpool's many facilities for letting people have fun.

The photographs in this *History Tour* allow a glimpse of parts of Blackpool at various times over the last 130 years or so. There have been some excellent developments in the town in recent years including the works at St John's Square, St John's School, the Hounds Hill Shopping Development, coastal protection work between North Pier and Squires Gate Lane, the Tower Headland and the complete renewal and replacement of the tramway and tramcars. However, not all change has been progress and, too often, the sublime or just interesting has been replaced by something bland or downright awful. Blackpool, however, does strive to improve itself and it will always have its glorious natural assets of golden sands and a view of the sea. It is clear that it will continue to develop, rebuild and repackage itself as a holiday resort.

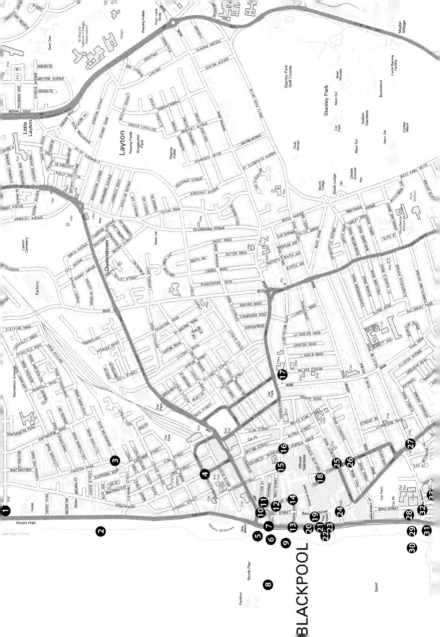

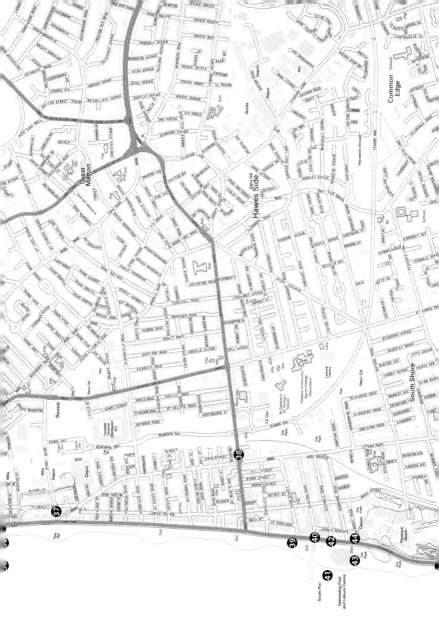

1. THE THREE PROMENADES, NORTH SHORE

The Claremont Park Estate from Cocker Street to the Gynn had been created in 1863 by the Blackpool Land, Building & Hotel Company and sea defence works were started in 1876 to protect Queen's Drive, the Imperial Hotel (1887) and other properties. The North Shore Works, between Cocker Square and the Gynn, and the three promenades were constructed in the period 1895–99. The colonnades and promenade widening works were completed in 1925. They allowed the tram tracks to be moved from the road to a separate reservation and also provided a long, covered walkway with seating facing the sea. The Middle Walk was for many years the location for events such as the finish of the 'Milk Race' and vintage bus and car rallies.

THREE PROMENADES, BLACKPOOL N.S.

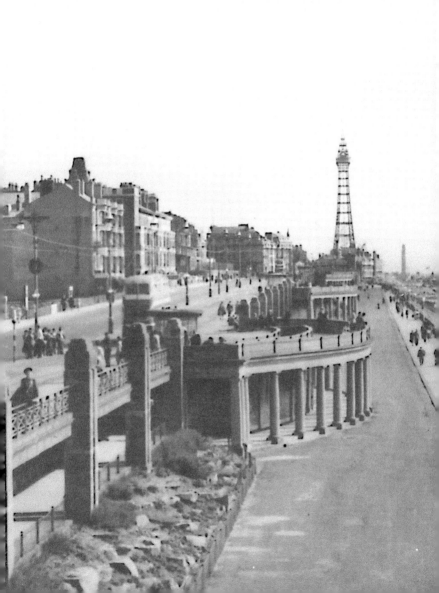

2. CLAREMONT PARK ESTATE

Claremont Park Estate, between Cocker Square and the Gynn, was developed from 1863. It is depicted here in a watercolour by the Lakeland artist W. T. Longmire dated 1868 when the Imperial Hotel, on the right, was but a year old. In the distance is Uncle Tom's Cabin on the Bispham cliffs. To the left is the Lower Walk, where there is now a Lower and Middle Promenade with colonnades. The twin tram tracks to Gynn Square were opened in 1900, after the Corporation took control of the once private frontage.

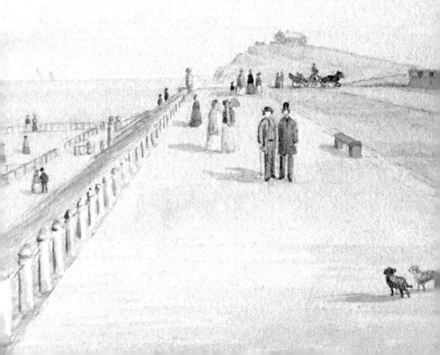

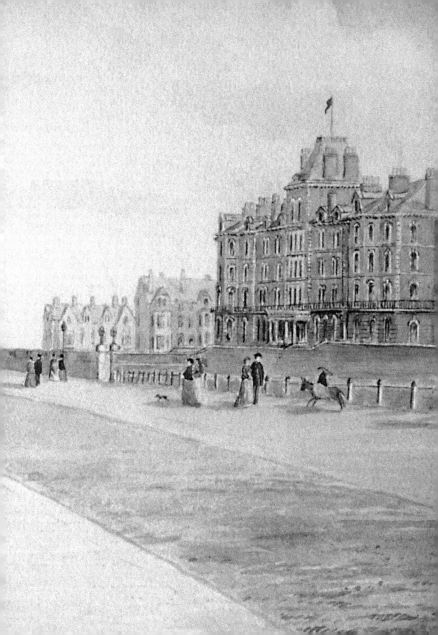

3. ASHBURTON ROAD

Ashburton Road is seen here, *c.* 1910, when it ended at Fielding's brickworks and builder's yard. Fielding built many properties at North Shore in the early twentieth century and Fielding Road is named after him. On the left corner of Egerton Road is the Ebenezer Methodist church, which opened on 25 May 1900 and was pulled down in 1982. On the right is Ashburton Road Council School of 1904, which was the school's dentist in the 1960s. The houses to the right were, for a long time, a launderette and sweet shop.

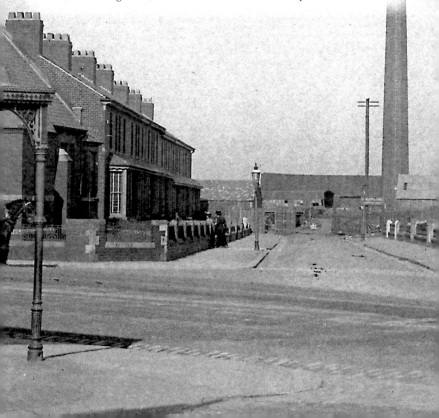

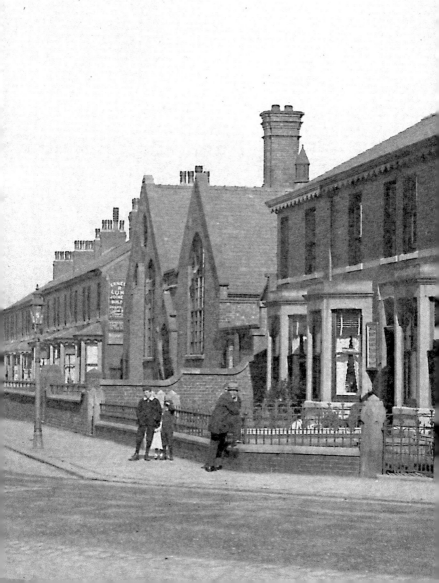

4. DICKSON ROAD

This view of a traffic- and tram-free Dickson Road looking north from near Springfield Road dates from around 1910. The terminus of the Blackpool & Fleetwood Electric Tramroad Co. was just behind this view and the passing loop of the single line tram track going north to Fleetwood via the Gynn can be seen in the road. To the right is Banks Street Unitarian church, which was opened in 1883 and closed as a church in 1975. Further along on the right is Dickson Road's Grade II listed Wesleyan Methodist church, built in 1907.

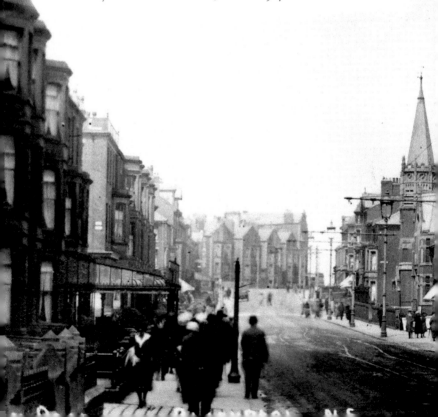

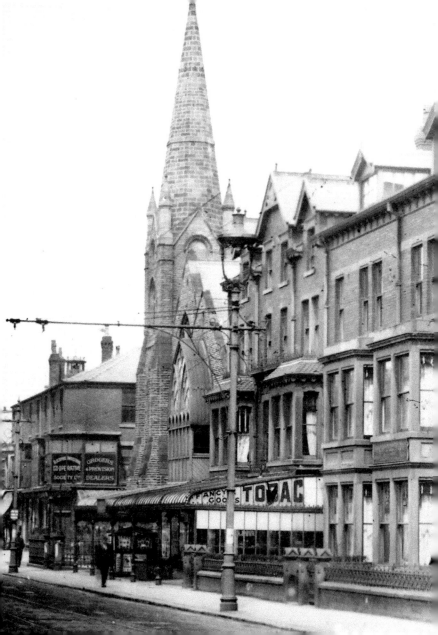

5. METROPOLE HOTEL

The Metropole Hotel was originally Bailey's Hotel, one of Blackpool's oldest hotels dating from the mid-1780s. The hotel became Dickson's in the 1840s and later Bailey's again. It is seen here in the early 1900s, looking north from North Pier before Princess Parade was constructed.

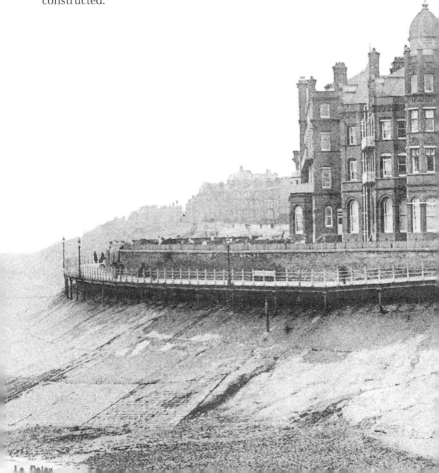

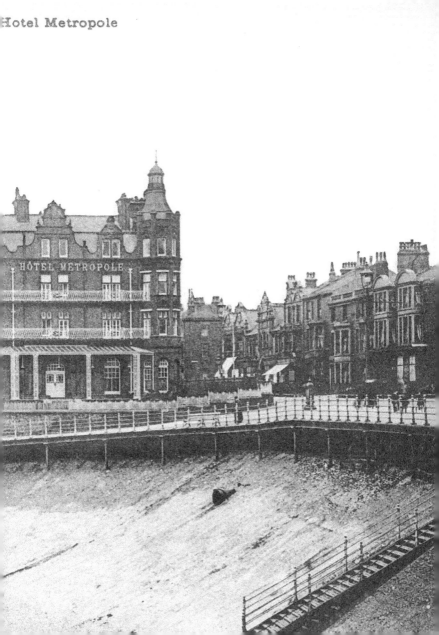

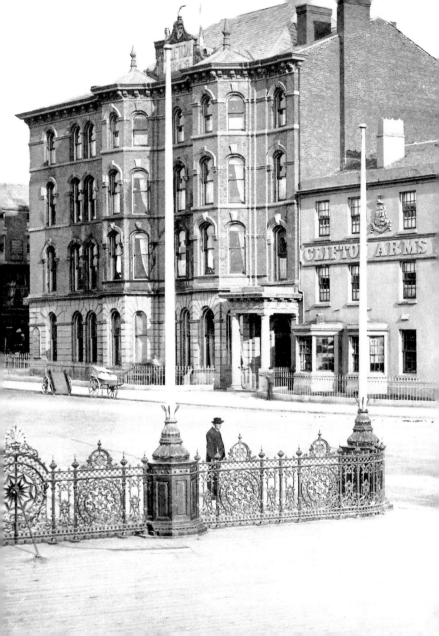

6. THE CLIFTON ARMS HOTEL IN THE 1870s

Originally this would have been a view of Forshaw's Hotel, one of Blackpool's first lodging places, built around 1780 on the corner of what is now Talbot Square and the Promenade. Forshaw's was sold to Thomas Clifton in 1843 and was reconstructed and replaced by the four-storey Grade II listed Clifton Hotel in the period 1865 to 1874. It is seen here from inside the cast-iron gates of North Pier in the 1870s, before the reconstruction of the north-west corner of the hotel had been completed.

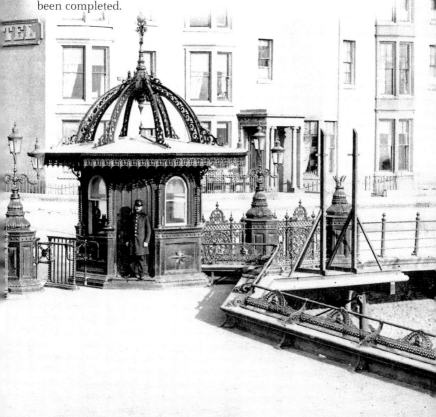

7. NORTH PIER

North Pier, Blackpool's first pier, was built by the Blackpool Pier Co. and opened on 21 May 1863. The pier as originally constructed was a simple but elegant structure intended for 'promenading'. A jetty was added in 1868, a new entrance was built in 1869 and the deck was widened in 1896. In 1903, new entrances, shops and an arcade were added to the shoreward end. The pier is seen here around 1905 when the ticket price was 2d. The Merrie England bar was opened in the mid-1960s and the pier was given a Victorian-style entrance twenty years later. The pier is now owned by a Blackpool family firm, the Sedgwicks.

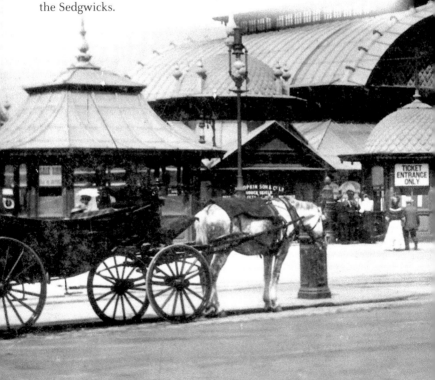

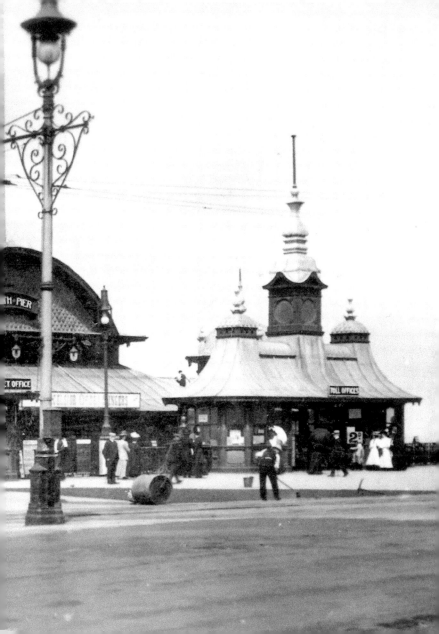

8. TOWER AND PROMENADE FROM NORTH PIER

This 1940s postcard view of the Promenade taken from North Pier shows, from left to right: Robert's Oyster Rooms; the modern Savoy Café building opened in 1937; Burton's Buildings, where the Albion Hotel had previously been until 1925; the County & Lane Ends Hotel at the bottom of Church Street (now Harry Ramsden's); the Palace, which was Lewis's from 1964 until it closed in 1993; the Tower; Woolworth's with its clock tower nearing completion; and the tourist information centre and toilets on the west side of the tram tracks.

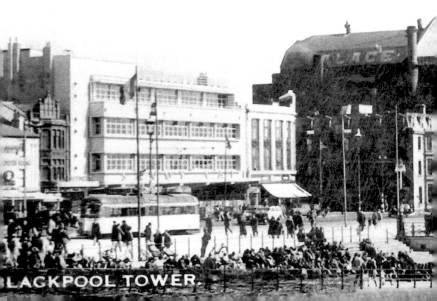

BLACKPOOL TOWER.

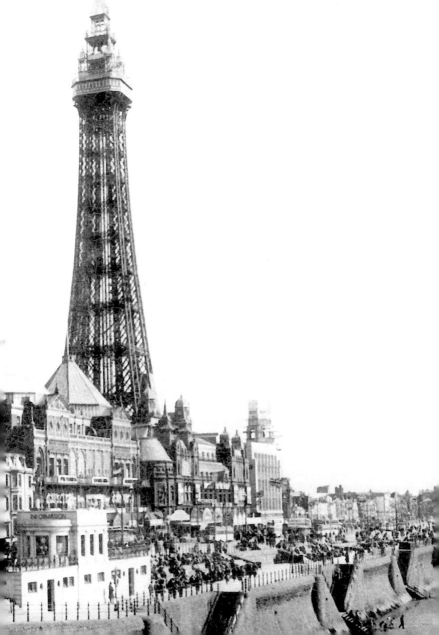

9. NORTH PIER

North Pier is seen here in the 1860s. It was designed by Eugenius Birch for the Blackpool Pier Co. Ltd. The pier opened on 21 May 1863 and was constructed using cast-iron screw piles and columns supporting wrought-iron girders and a timber deck. Originally, the promenade deck was 1,070 feet long and only 28 feet wide. The beach with the bathing huts was more inclined in the 1860s and still had many pebbles and gravel.

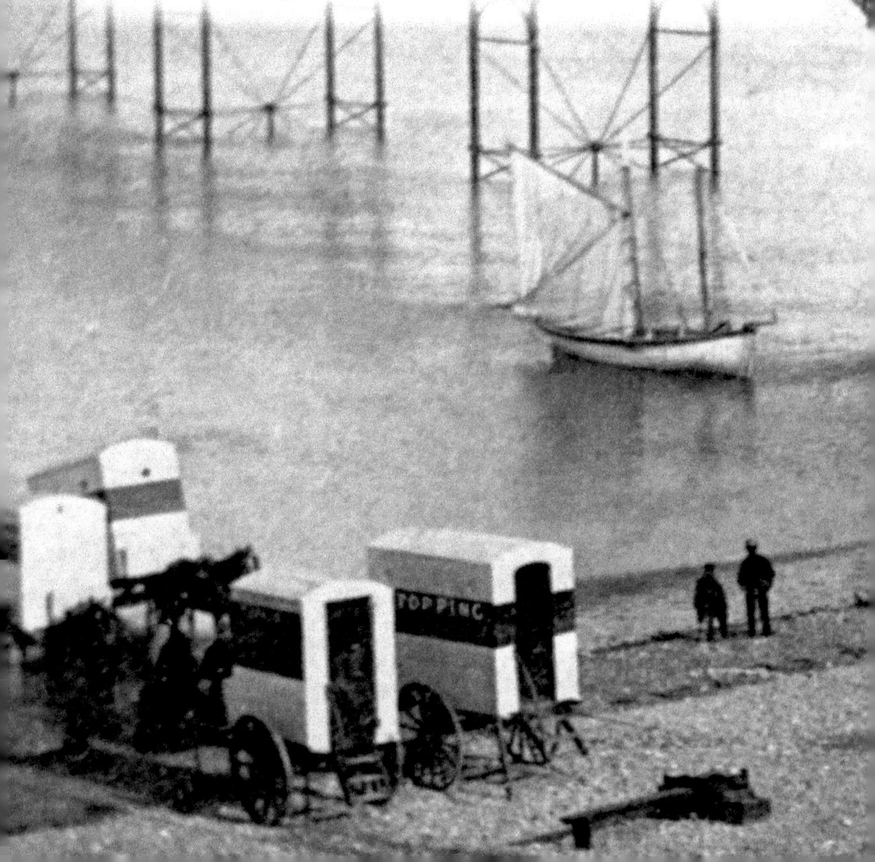

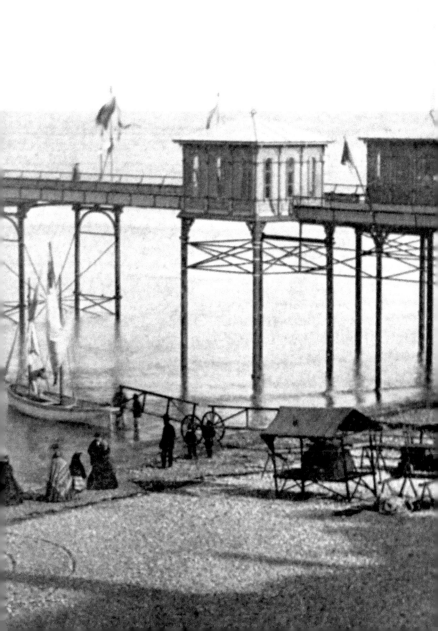

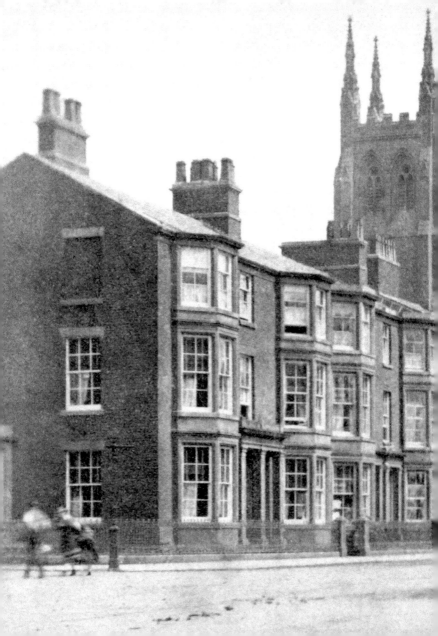

10. TALBOT ROAD

This is the view looking up Talbot Road from Talbot Square in the mid-1860s. The houses in the foreground soon became shop premises, the best known being a café run for many years by the Jenkinson sisters; this became the Movenpick in the 1960s, then Jenk's Bar and later Rumours night spot. Sacred Heart RC church (*centre*) opened in 1857, and beyond is Viener's Bazaar, which opened in 1859. Apart from wooden huts, the photograph shows only one building between the Railway Hotel and Talbot Road station.

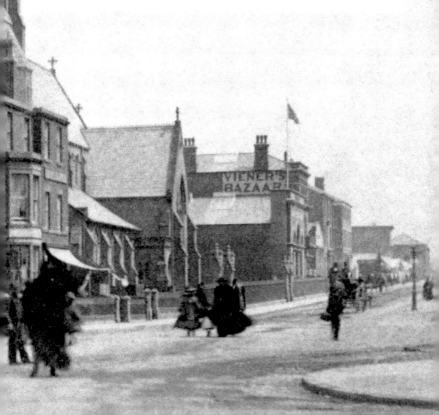

11. CLIFTON STREET

Looking up Clifton Street towards the new General Post Office on Abingdon Street, a 'toastrack' tram can be seen on the circular tour that had taken it along the Promenade to South Shore, before returning via Waterloo Road, Whitegate Drive and Church Street. The photograph dates from around 1912, when some of the boarding houses were already becoming shop premises. Now building societies and restaurants predominate.

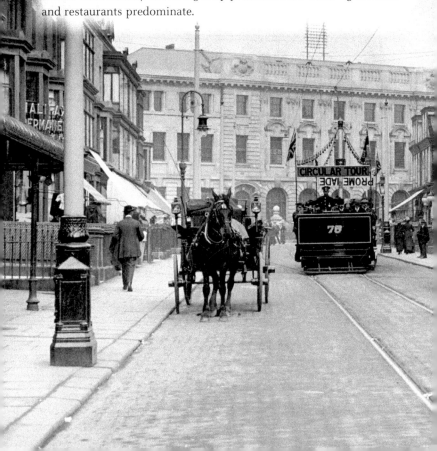

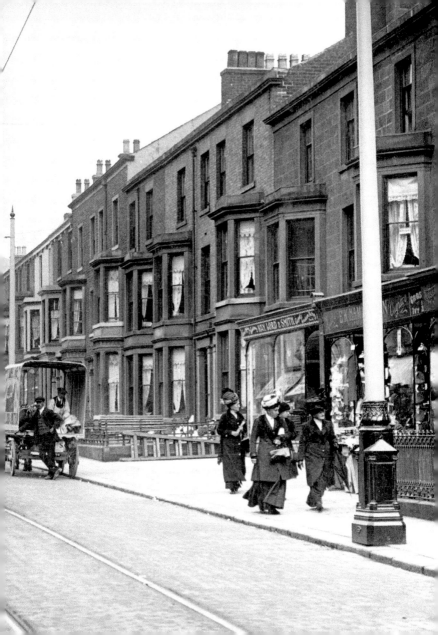

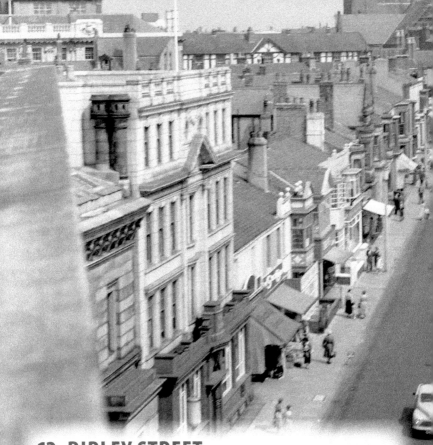

12. BIRLEY STREET

Birley Street, seen in July 1959 from the roof of the Municipal Buildings before the Crown Hotel, on the right, was rebuilt in 1963. The street was pedestrianised in 1996 and from 2009 has been dominated by the arguably over-engineered 'Brilliance' light display, which is somewhat reminiscent of some giant stainless steel mudguards having been deposited there.

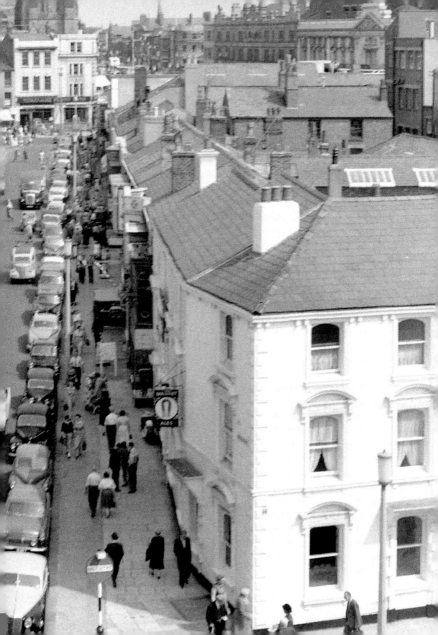

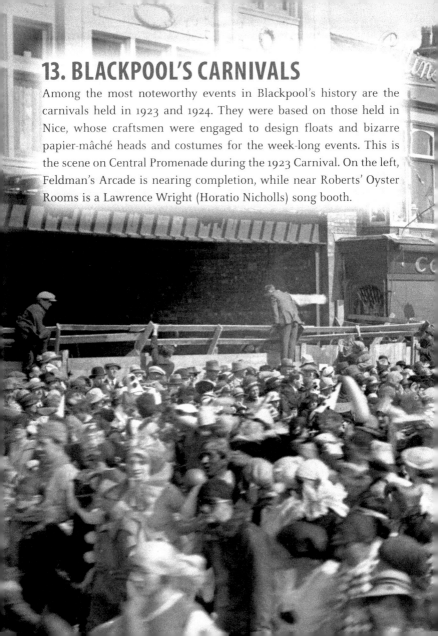

13. BLACKPOOL'S CARNIVALS

Among the most noteworthy events in Blackpool's history are the carnivals held in 1923 and 1924. They were based on those held in Nice, whose craftsmen were engaged to design floats and bizarre papier-mâché heads and costumes for the week-long events. This is the scene on Central Promenade during the 1923 Carnival. On the left, Feldman's Arcade is nearing completion, while near Roberts' Oyster Rooms is a Lawrence Wright (Horatio Nicholls) song booth.

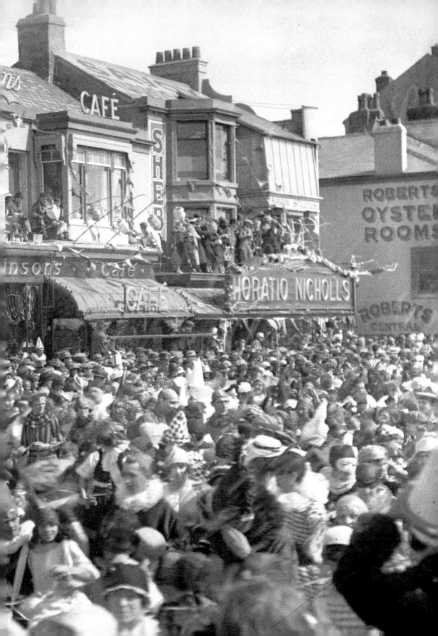

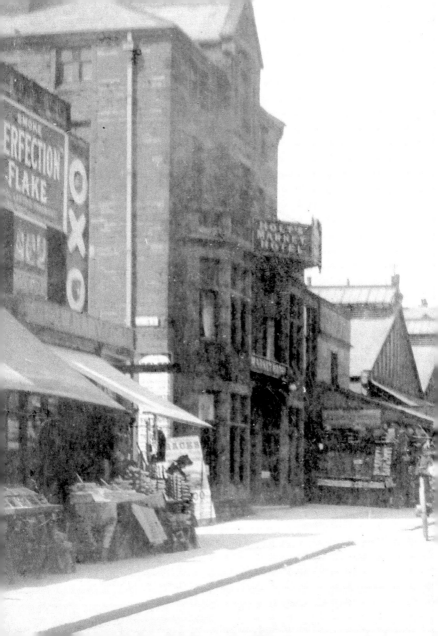

14. CORPORATION STREET

Corporation Street was originally named Lytham Street and is seen here from near Church Street around 1905. To the left is Euston Street. The block of property, bounded by Church Street, Market Street, Corporation Street and West Street, which included Euston Street, was demolished in 1939. This site was largely vacant until British Home Stores was built, opening in May 1957. Just beyond Euston Street is the Market Hotel and further up is the St John's Market extension. In the distance is the town hall, completed in 1900, with its spire, which was demolished in 1966. Birley Street is on the right.

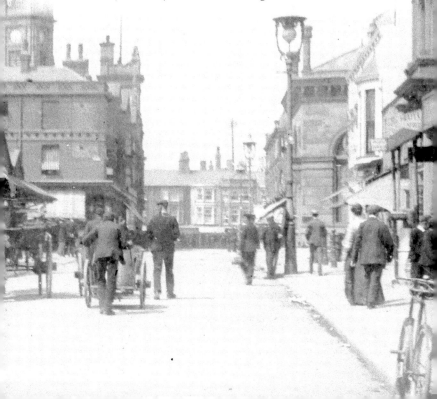

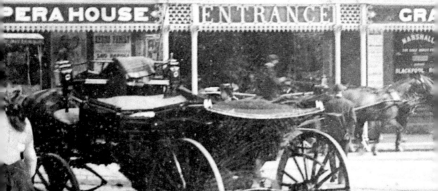

15. THE WINTER GARDENS, CHURCH STREET

The Winter Gardens was built on the Bank Hey Estate of Dr Cocker, the first Mayor of Blackpool. An open-air skating rink was opened in July 1876. Two years later, the main entrance, with a 120-foot-high glazed dome, the floral hall and the pavilion also opened. The first Opera House was added in 1889, while the huge Empress Ballroom dates from 1896. The Winter Gardens has hosted the annual conferences for all of the main British political parties and has been the home of the Blackpool Dance Festival since 1920. The complex was purchased by Blackpool Council from Leisure Parcs Ltd in 2010.

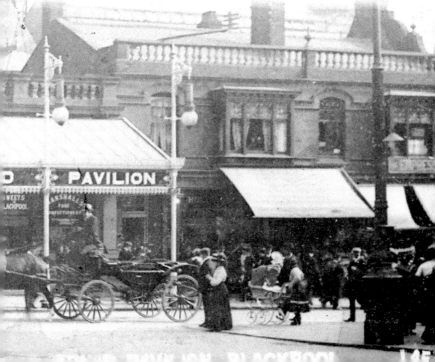

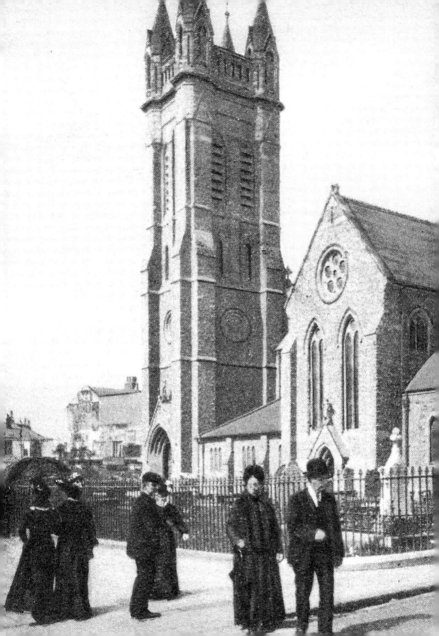

16. ST JOHN'S CHURCH, CHURCH STREET

Blackpool's first church was the Church of St John the Evangelist near what is now the corner of Abingdon Street and Church Street. It was consecrated on 6 July 1821 and demolished in 1877 to be replaced by the present parish church, which was consecrated on 25 June 1878. Its interior has recently been partitioned to create new rooms for both church and community use. The area of Church Street around the church has now been transformed from a busy through route to a well-designed pedestrianised piazza known as St John's Square. The focal point of the square is a 10½-metre-high steel sculpture with diving figure and illuminated resin inserts named *The Wave*, installed in September 2009 just before the square was officially opened.

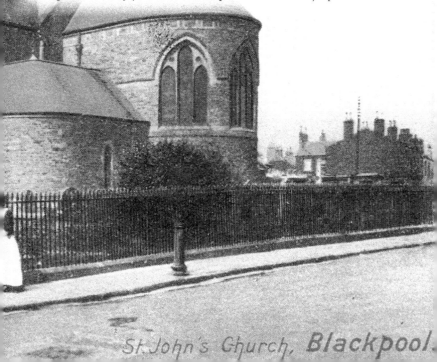

St John's Church, Blackpool.

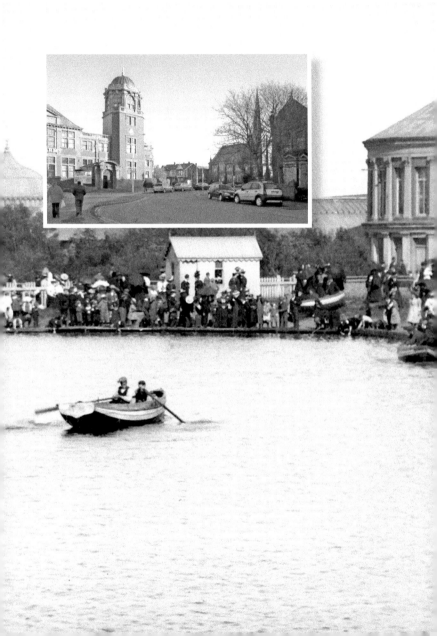

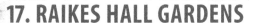
17. RAIKES HALL GARDENS

Raikes Hall Gardens is seen here in the 1890s, with its boating lake, grandstand and theatre. From the mid-1890s its future was in doubt and, despite suggestions that it should become a public park, in 1896 land at its perimeter was sold for building. Its last full season was in 1901, but in November its lake was drained and the following year new streets were laid out.

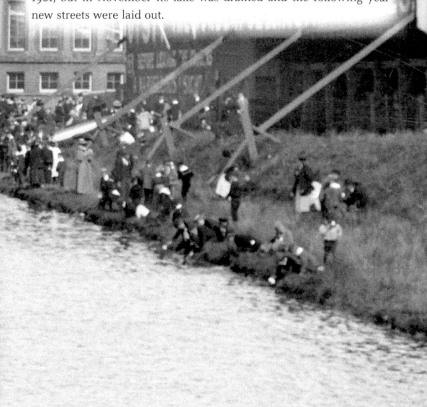

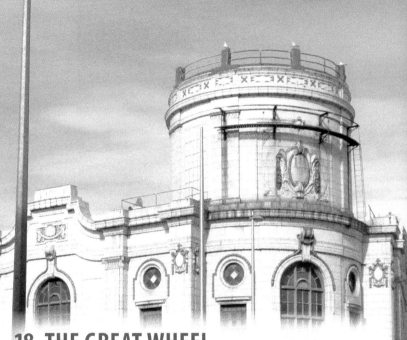

18. THE GREAT WHEEL, CORONATION STREET

The entrance to the Great Wheel, which was 200 feet in diameter, was on the corner of Coronation Street and Adelaide Street, now the site of the Olympia. The Great Wheel opened on 22 August 1896 and had thirty carriages, each capable of holding thirty passengers. Purchased by the Winter Gardens Company in 1916 for £1,150, it closed on 20 October 1928 and its carriages were sold off at auction for £13 each. Tower Street is to the left of the old view from around 1910 but the block of properties between Tower Street and Coronation Street were demolished in late 2010.

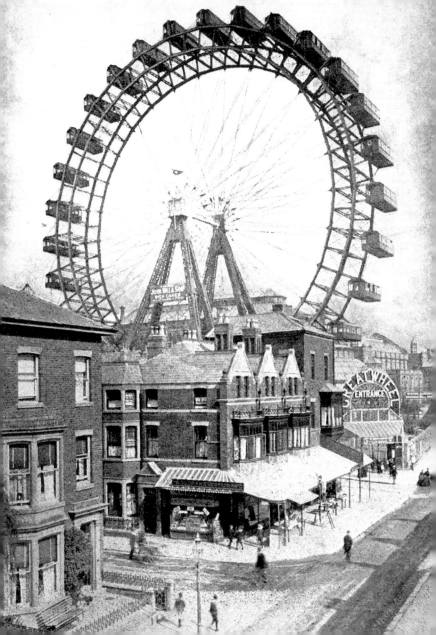

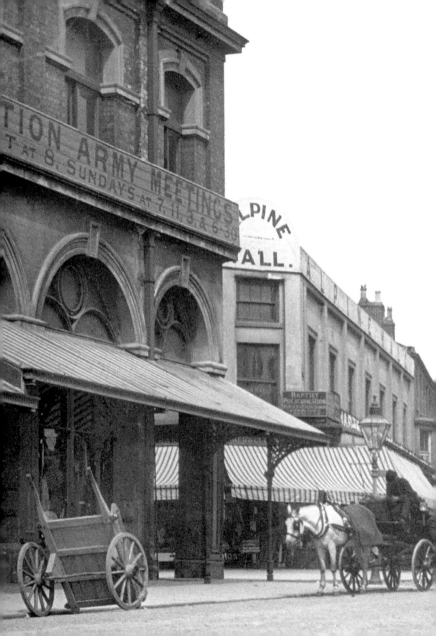

19. VICTORIA STREET

This is the view up Victoria Street from the Promenade around 1890, with the original Victoria Street entrance to the Winter Gardens in the distance. On the extreme left is the Prince of Wales Theatre and Market. Just beyond it is what is labelled as the Alpine Hall. The building opened in 1837, on what was then Green Walk, as the Victoria Promenade, Blackpool's first public assembly hall, which had seven shop units below. It survived until 2000, when the property was rebuilt.

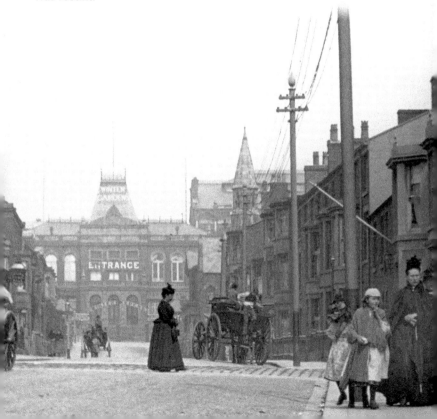

20. THE PALACE

This site was originally a row of houses named Hygiene Terrace. It was replaced by the Prince of Wales Theatre (1877) and Baths (1881), which themselves were replaced by the Alhambra in May 1899. The Alhambra had a magnificent entrance hall and a 'conservatory' on the top floor, together with a circus, theatre and ballroom. It was not a financial success and the building was acquired by the Blackpool Tower Co., remodelled and reopened as the Palace in 1904. In 1935 the cost of the Variety & Revue show ranged from 1s to 2s 6d. Lewis' department store, with its distinctive 'honeycomb' front façade, traded on the site from 1964 to 1993, and the site is now occupied by a variety of shops.

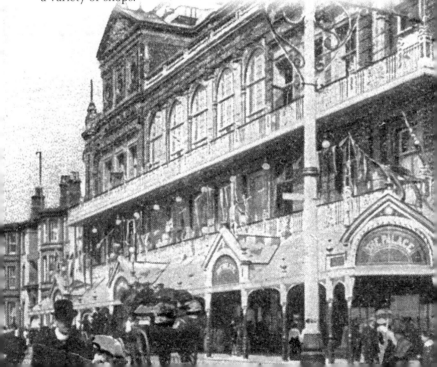

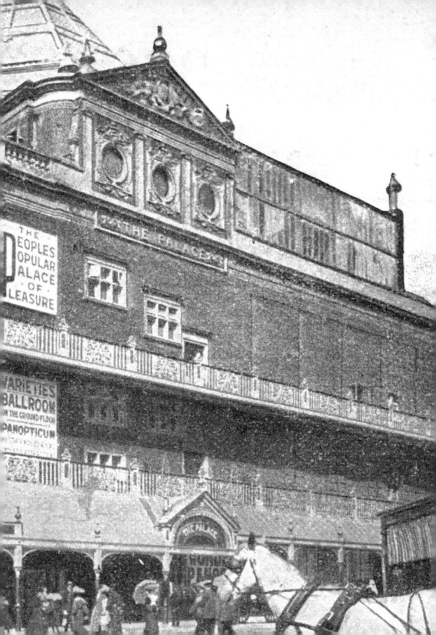

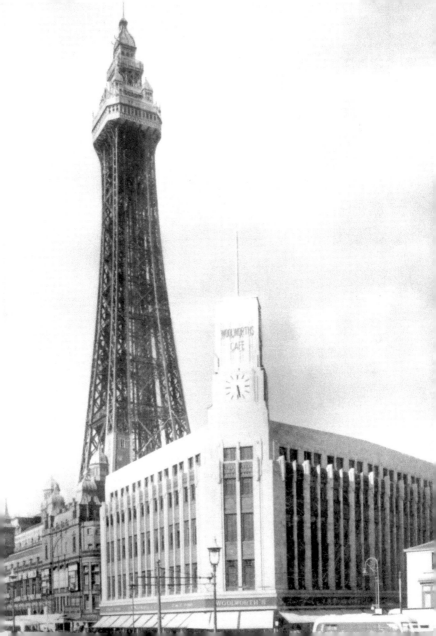

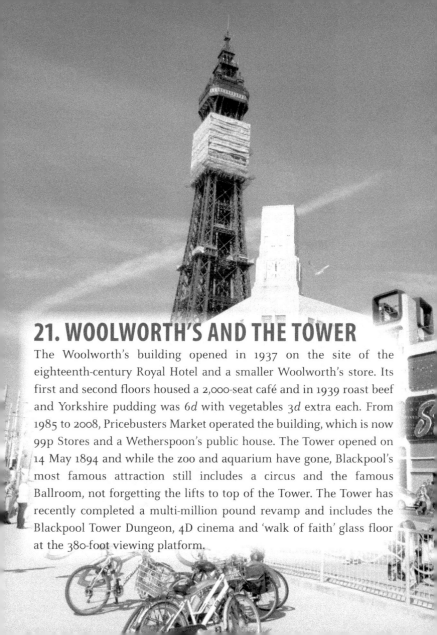

21. WOOLWORTH'S AND THE TOWER

The Woolworth's building opened in 1937 on the site of the eighteenth-century Royal Hotel and a smaller Woolworth's store. Its first and second floors housed a 2,000-seat café and in 1939 roast beef and Yorkshire pudding was 6*d* with vegetables 3*d* extra each. From 1985 to 2008, Pricebusters Market operated the building, which is now 99p Stores and a Wetherspoon's public house. The Tower opened on 14 May 1894 and while the zoo and aquarium have gone, Blackpool's most famous attraction still includes a circus and the famous Ballroom, not forgetting the lifts to top of the Tower. The Tower has recently completed a multi-million pound revamp and includes the Blackpool Tower Dungeon, 4D cinema and 'walk of faith' glass floor at the 380-foot viewing platform.

22. THE PROMENADE

The Central Promenade looking north from the Palatine Hotel in the late 1880s. A few years later the Tower would dominate Blackpool seafront.

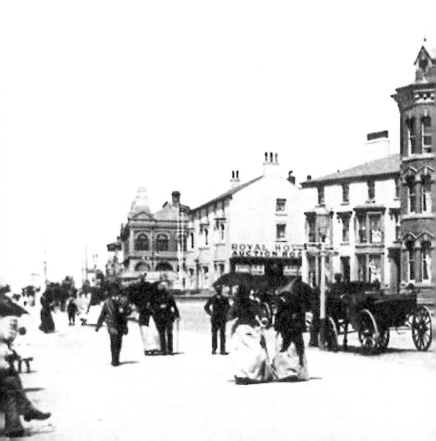

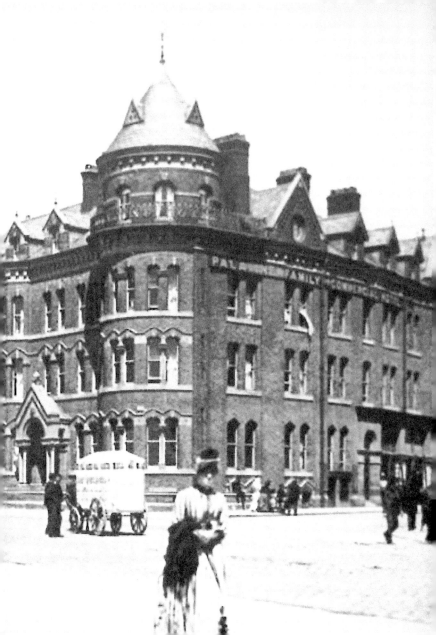

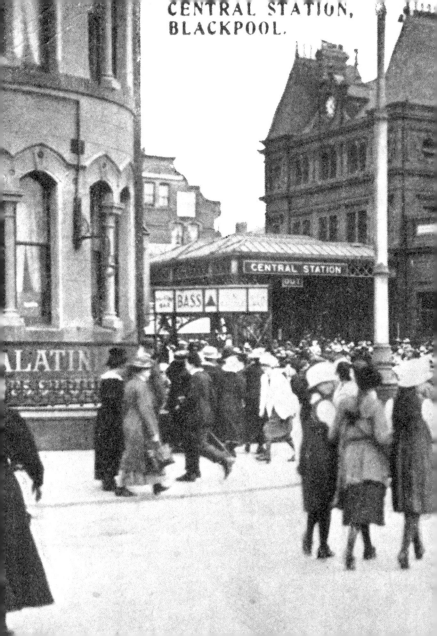

CENTRAL STATION,
BLACKPOOL.

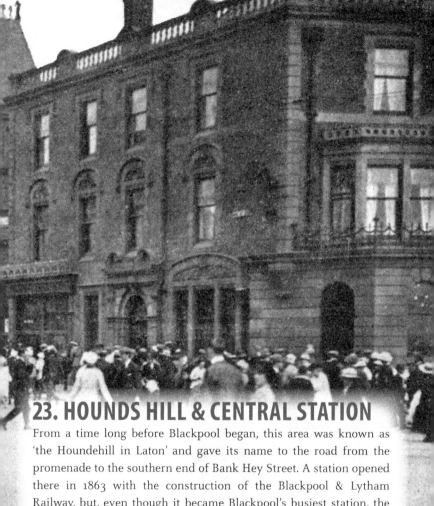

23. HOUNDS HILL & CENTRAL STATION

From a time long before Blackpool began, this area was known as 'the Houndehill in Laton' and gave its name to the road from the promenade to the southern end of Bank Hey Street. A station opened there in 1863 with the construction of the Blackpool & Lytham Railway, but, even though it became Blackpool's busiest station, the line closed in 1964, largely due to the development potential of the station land and the sidings to the south. The New Inn & Central Hotel building is to the right. The site of the station and New Inn was redeveloped in the late 1970s as the Coral Island amusement complex.

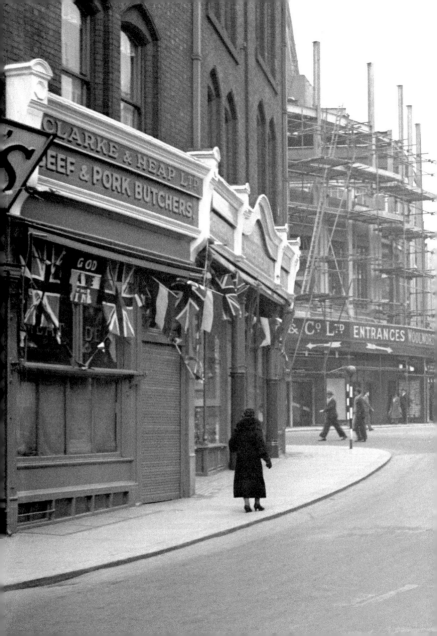

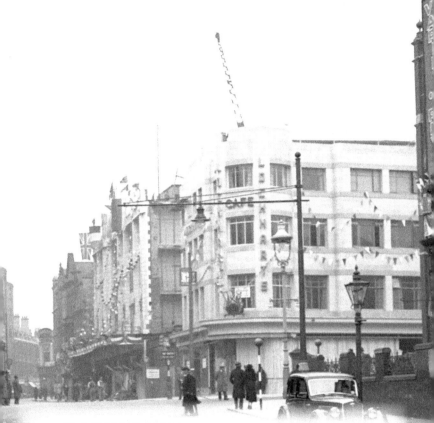

24. HOUNDS HILL

Hounds Hill, looking north towards Bank Hey Street in 1937, when the Art Deco Woolworth's superstore was being built next to the Tower. Opposite, a modernist styled Lockhart's Café had recently been completed and, next to it, work had begun on the last extension of R. H. O. Hill's department store. In the foreground on the left is the Palatine Hotel block.

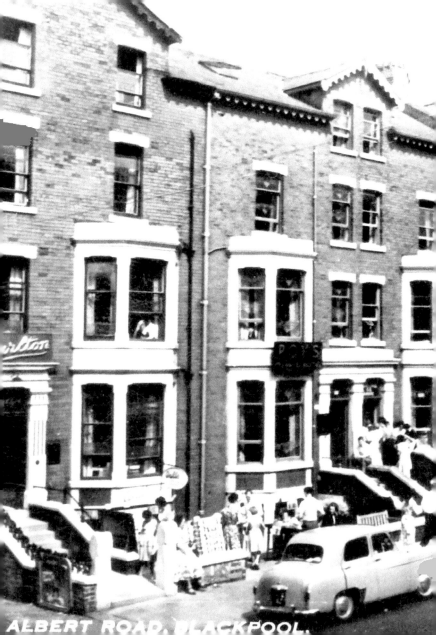

ALBERT ROAD, BLACKPOOL.

25. ALBERT ROAD

The hotel and guesthouse properties of Albert Road have changed little, except that many have acquired front 'lounge' extensions and some have been extended upwards with 'roof lifts'. The cars in this 1950s photograph would all now be classics, and it shows the two-way road before traffic management was invented.

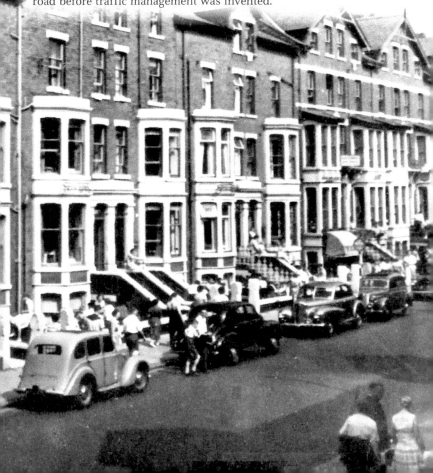

26. HULL ROAD

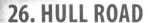

The taking of a street photograph was obviously quite an occasion in the early 1900s in the cobbled Hull Road between Coronation Street and Central Drive. The guesthouse properties in Hull Road, to whom these photographs would be sold so that guests could send home pictures of where they had stayed, were ideally placed to capitalise on the millions of holidaymakers who flowed out of the Central station terminus (seen in the distance at the bottom of the road) and the proximity of the Tower, the Promenade and the town centre.

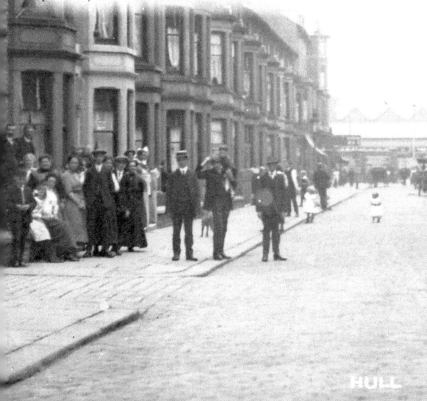

HULL

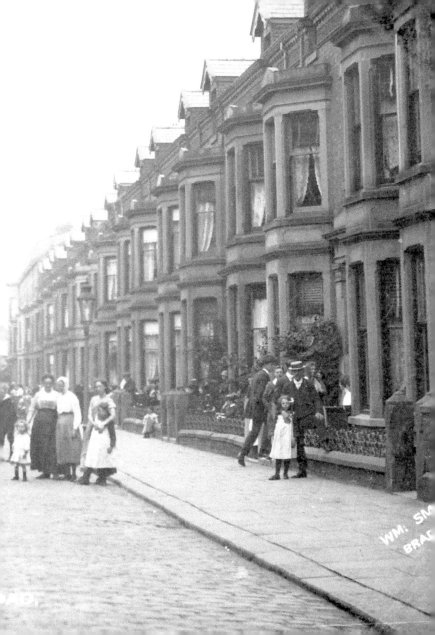

WM. SM
BRAD

View of Central Drive, Blackpool

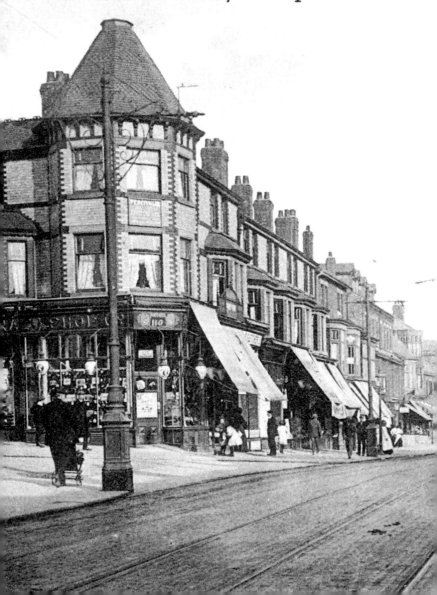

27. CENTRAL DRIVE LOOKING SOUTH FROM CHAPEL STREET

In 1882, Central Drive ran as far as Revoe Farm (near the site of Revoe Library). This view from around 1905 is looking south into the Revoe area of Blackpool, with Palatine Road on the left, the George Hotel (1893) in the distant centre and Revoe Library further away. It shows how, as a result of the rapid expansion of Blackpool, little remained of the farmland in this area. The tram tracks of the 'Marton Loop' can be seen; the line opened in 1901 and was discontinued in 1936.

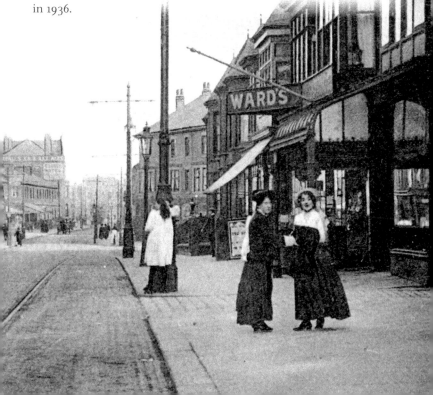

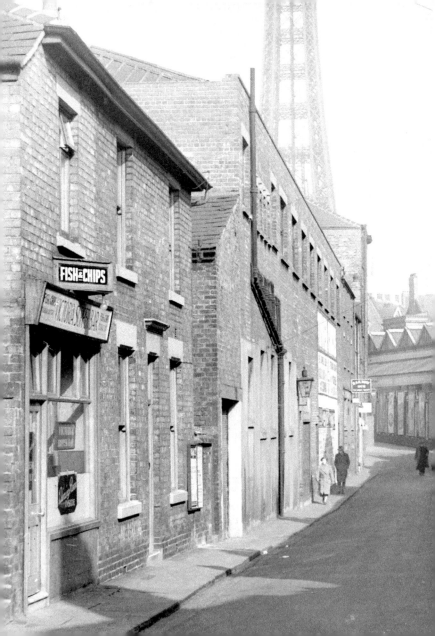

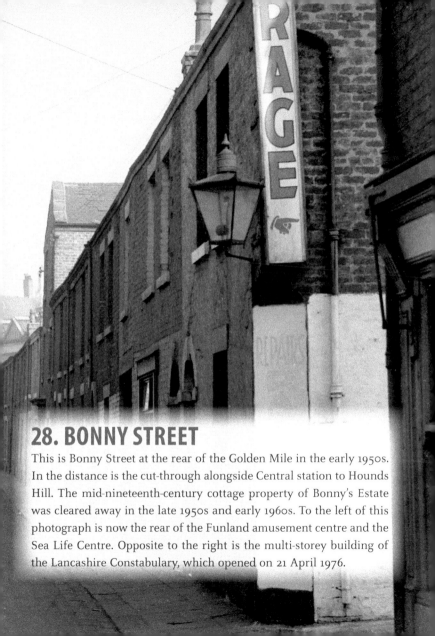

28. BONNY STREET

This is Bonny Street at the rear of the Golden Mile in the early 1950s. In the distance is the cut-through alongside Central station to Hounds Hill. The mid-nineteenth-century cottage property of Bonny's Estate was cleared away in the late 1950s and early 1960s. To the left of this photograph is now the rear of the Funland amusement centre and the Sea Life Centre. Opposite to the right is the multi-storey building of the Lancashire Constabulary, which opened on 21 April 1976.

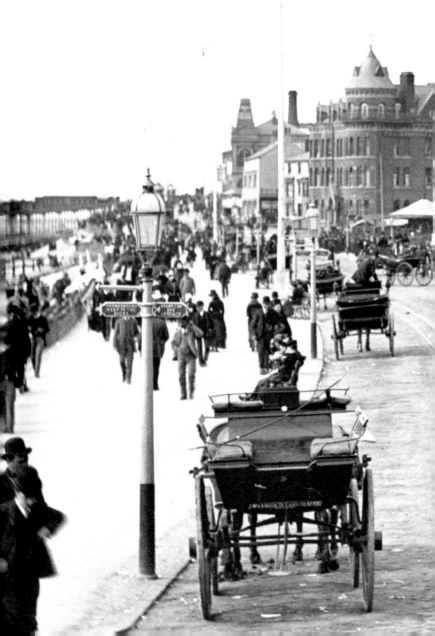

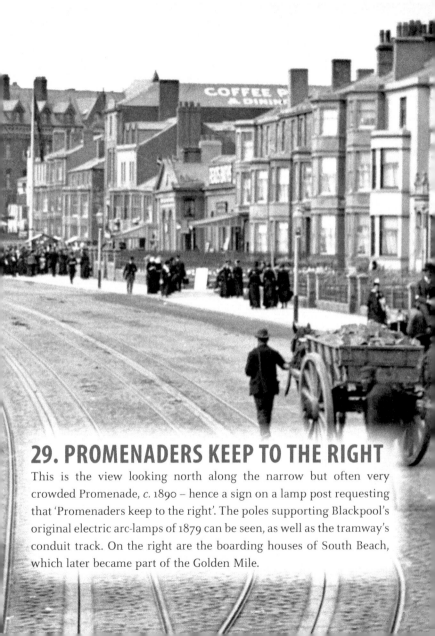

29. PROMENADERS KEEP TO THE RIGHT

This is the view looking north along the narrow but often very crowded Promenade, *c.* 1890 – hence a sign on a lamp post requesting that 'Promenaders keep to the right'. The poles supporting Blackpool's original electric arc-lamps of 1879 can be seen, as well as the tramway's conduit track. On the right are the boarding houses of South Beach, which later became part of the Golden Mile.

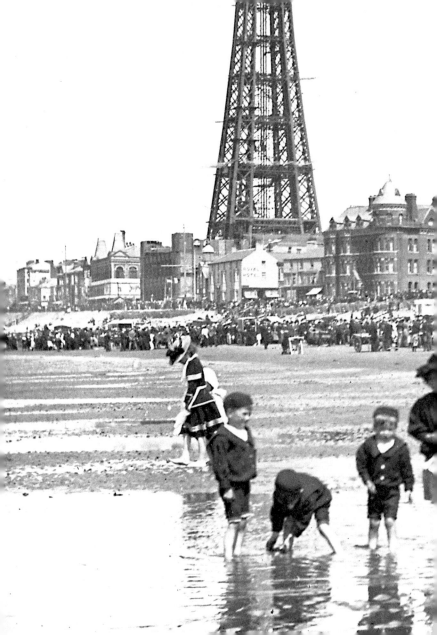

30. THE BEACH

A view taken from the beach during the summer of 1893 is shown, when work on the Tower structure had reached 380 feet, the level of the first viewing platform. Of the buildings in this photograph, the Tower is the only survivor along this section of the Promenade as far north as Church Street.

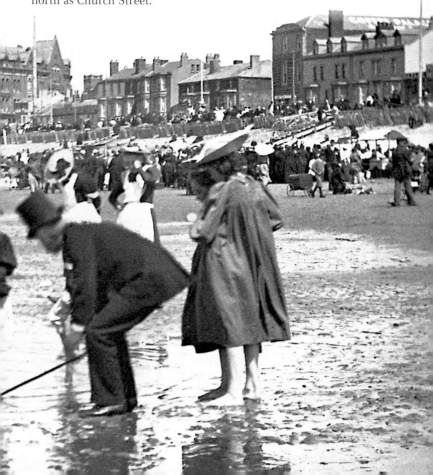

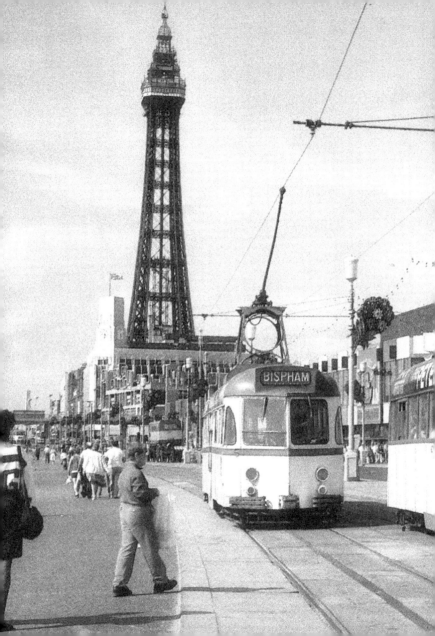

31. TRAMS, CENTRAL PROMENADE

In this 1970s view, two Brush Cars dating from 1937 are seen passing on Central Promenade. Brush Car 627 was previously (pre-1968) numbered 290 and was the last car to run on the North station line. This car is now owned by the Fleetwood Heritage Leisure Trust and has been restored and painted in white and gold for the Queen's Diamond Jubilee. The £100 million tramway improvement scheme included the replacement of 11 miles of track and the building of a new tram depot at Starr Gate. The new Bombardier Flexity 2 trams became operational on 4 April 2012.

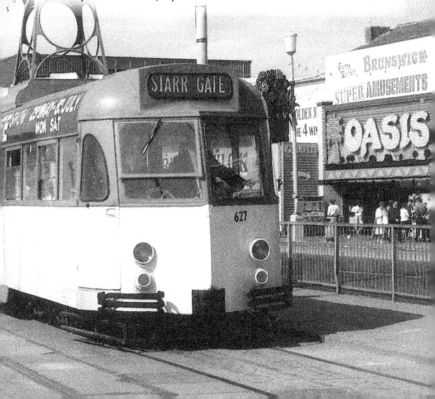

32. CHAPEL STREET

From medieval times, a track ran from Layton (near the No. 4 pub) to the sea along what is now the line of Chapel Street. This almost traffic-free 1920s photograph shows the properties that were demolished in the 1960s to make way for the road widening and building of the car park and courts. The Stanley Arms building on the right survives and is now Ma Kelly's Show Bar. The red-brick building in the centre was the Primitive Methodist church, founded in 1876, and became the Blackpool Foyer, a support service for young single homeless people that opened in 1999.

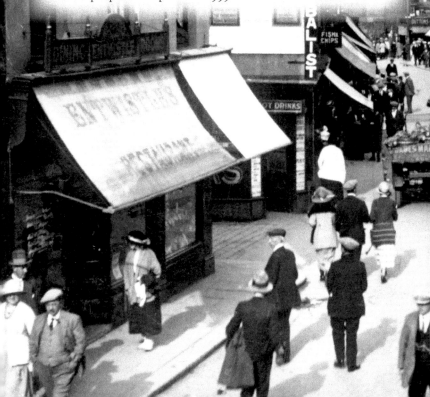

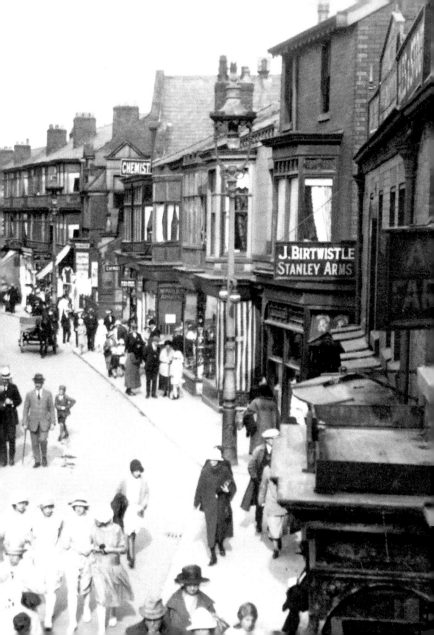

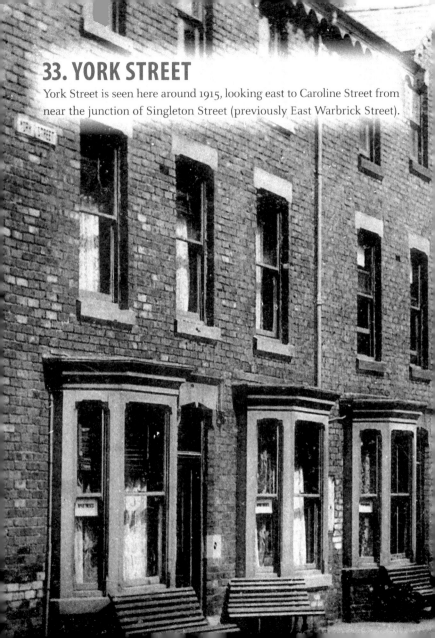

33. YORK STREET

York Street is seen here around 1915, looking east to Caroline Street from near the junction of Singleton Street (previously East Warbrick Street).

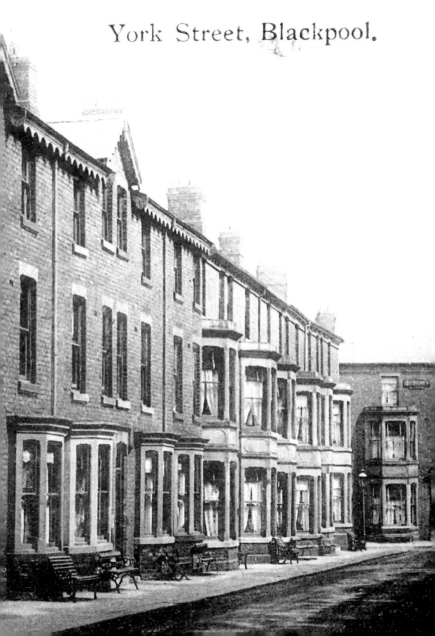

York Street, Blackpool.

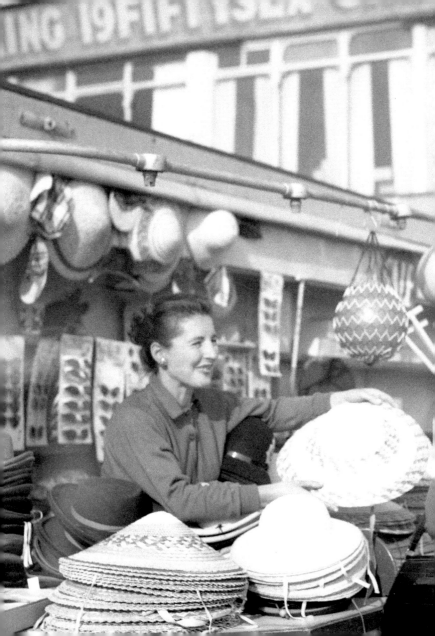

34. GOLDEN MILE

Despite being arguably improved by modern purpose-built amusement arcades, there is nostalgia for the former improvised and slightly ramshackle nature of the Golden Mile, which had arisen in the gardens of boarding houses of South Beach. It is perhaps typified by this photograph – apparently taken in 19FIFTYSEX! Something of the same character can still be found a little further south along the Promenade.

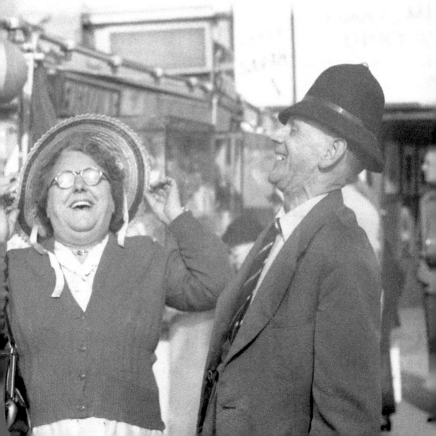

35. CENTRAL PIER

Here is a busy scene at the entrance to the Central Pier, *c.* 1932. This section of the promenade had been widened by 100 feet in 1904/05, allowing the tramway to be taken off the road.

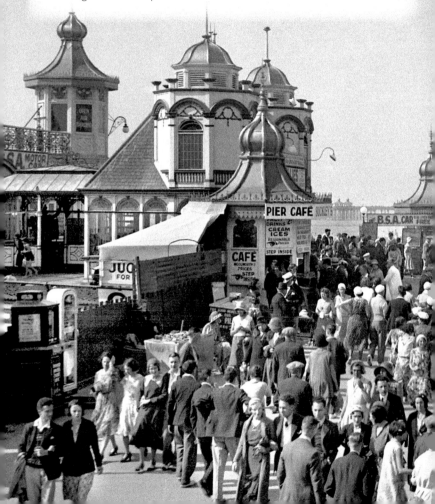

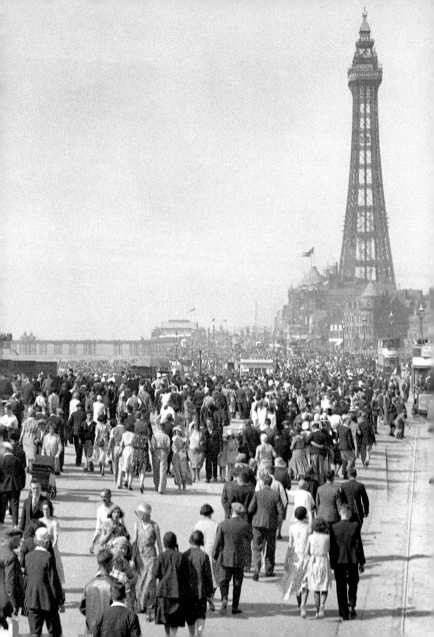

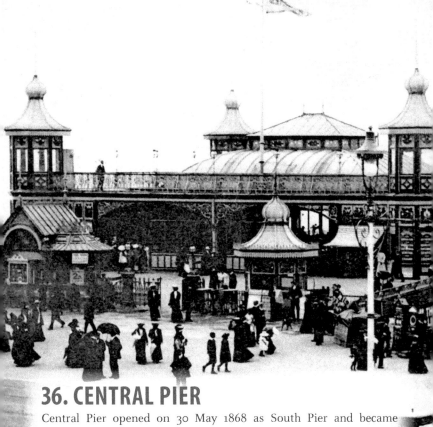

36. CENTRAL PIER

Central Pier opened on 30 May 1868 as South Pier and became known as 'The People's Pier' due to open-air dancing to a band. Its name changed to Central Pier in 1893 when the Victoria (South) Pier was opened. The pier is seen here around 1906 with its pavilion (1903). Amusement machines and rides were introduced in the early twentieth century. The pavilion was demolished in 1966 to make way for the Dixieland Bar, and in 1986 it became Maggie Mays. The 33-metre-high Ferris wheel was added in 1990.

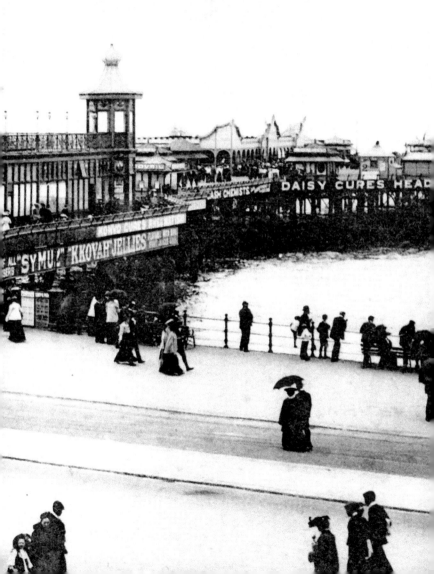

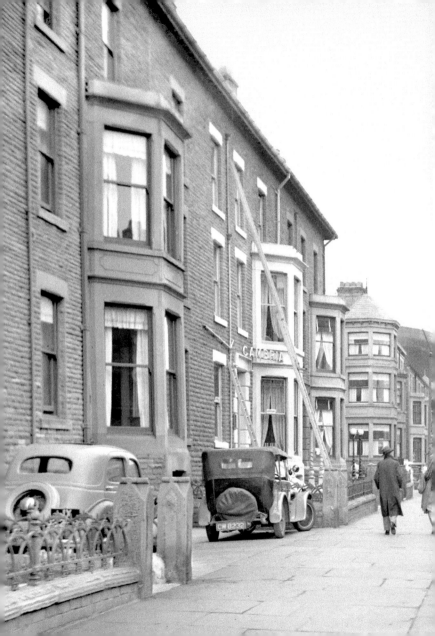

37. RIGBY ROAD

This is the view east along Rigby Road from the Promenade in the mid-1930s. On the right at the corner of Tyldesley Road is the Plaza Picture Theatre, which opened as the Royal Pavilion in 1909 as Blackpool's first purpose-built cinema. While it is not the most prepossessing early cinema building, it still exists as a fun bar.

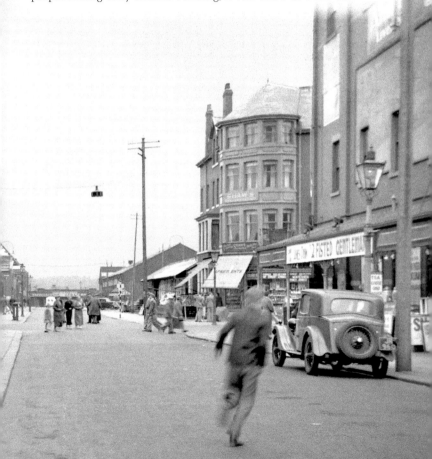

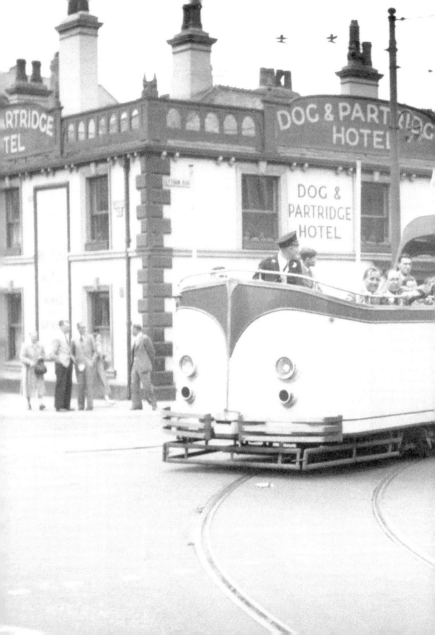

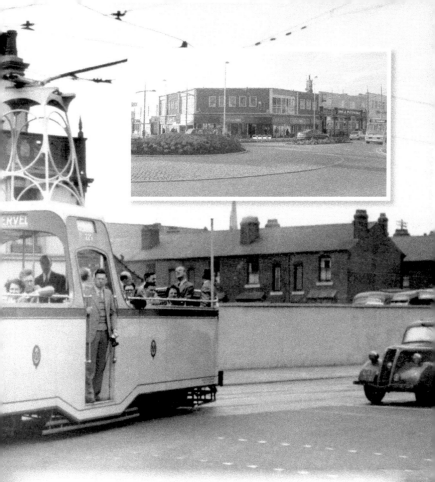

38. A BOAT TRAM

A boat tram carrying visiting tram enthusiasts is shown turning from Lytham Road into Waterloo Road by the Dog & Partridge in June 1954. The pub was rebuilt in 1959 and set further back.

39. QUEEN'S HYDRO HOTEL

Afternoon tea on the lawn of the Queen's Hydro Hotel, on an Edwardian summer's day, seems a far cry from manoeuvring in the tarmac car park of the Queen's Hotel, as it is now called. In 1882, the premises of what were once the Merchants College, and the College Français before it, had been enlarged to become the South Shore Hydropathic Establishment, which was developed into the Queen's Hydro Hotel in the late 1890s.

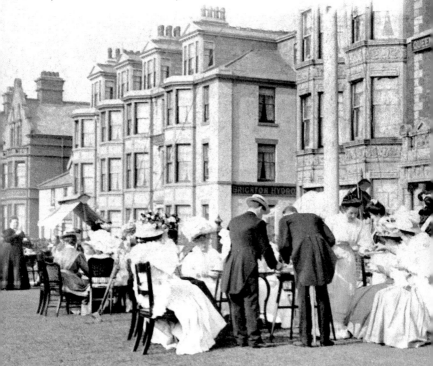

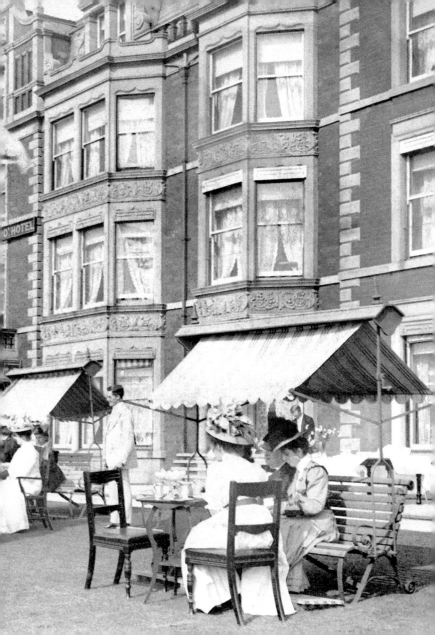

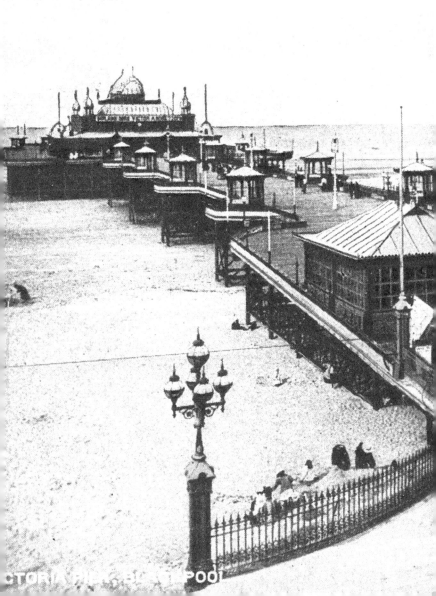

CTORIA PIER, BLACKPOOL

40. VICTORIA PIER (SOUTH PIER)

Victoria Pier, the third of Blackpool's piers, was built by the Blackpool South Shore Pier & Pavilion Co. Ltd in the rapidly developing South Shore area and opened on Good Friday 1893. At 489 feet in length, it is the shortest of the three piers. The Grand Pavilion held brass band and classical concerts and seasonal shows. It was destroyed by fire in 1958. The pier changed its name to South Pier in 1930 and amusement stalls and rides now predominate.

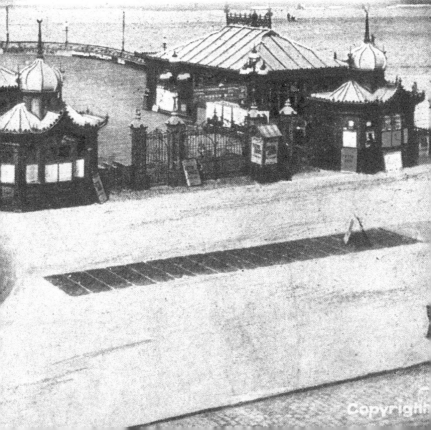

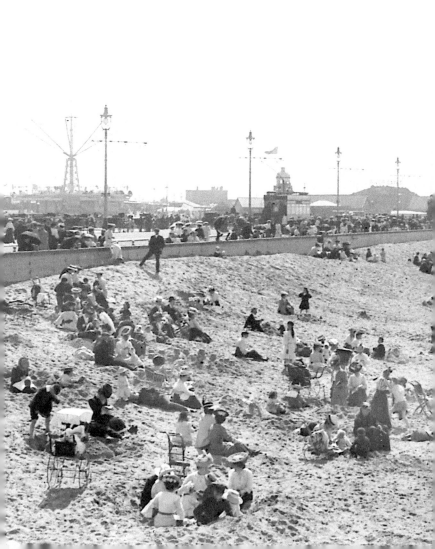

41. LOOKING SOUTH FROM VICTORIA PIER

This is the view looking south from Victoria (now South) Pier in 1906. At that time the Promenade ended at Balmoral Road, a convenient terminus for tram passengers wishing to visit the quickly evolving Pleasure Beach beyond. Its thrills already included the Captive Flying Machines, the Helter-Skelter Lighthouse, the River Caves, a Switchback Railway and the Sea Circus.

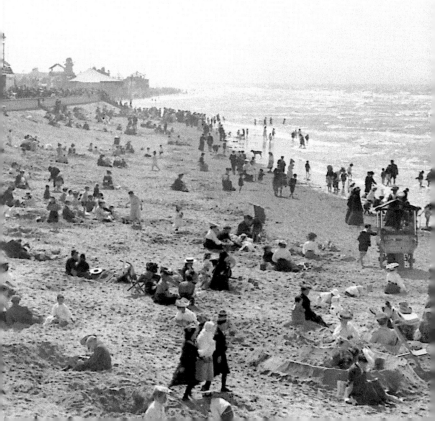

42. SOUTH PIER, LOOKING NORTH

This postcard view, posted in 1909, was taken following the widening of the entrance to Victoria Pier (South Pier) in 1902 and captures the popularity of strolling along the Promenade in hats and coats. At this time the trams terminated at the Pleasure Beach. They were extended to Starr Gate when the New South Promenade was opened in 1926.

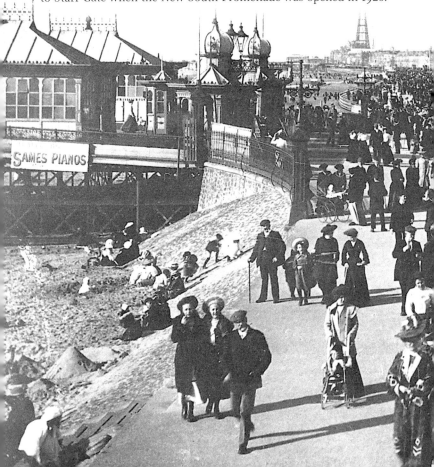

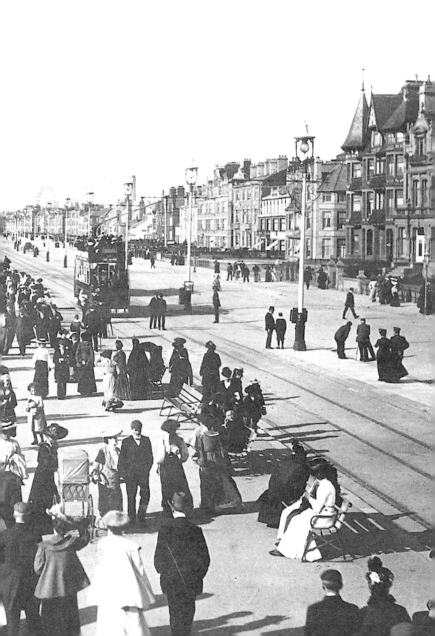

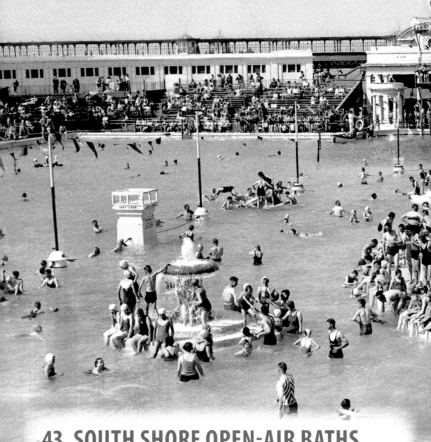

43. SOUTH SHORE OPEN-AIR BATHS

In June 1923, South Shore Open-Air Baths, the world's largest, opened on what had been the beach. The baths were demolished in March 1983 and the Sandcastle indoor water centre opened on the site in 1986.

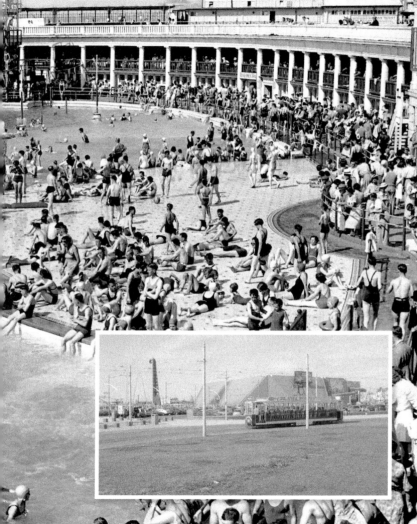

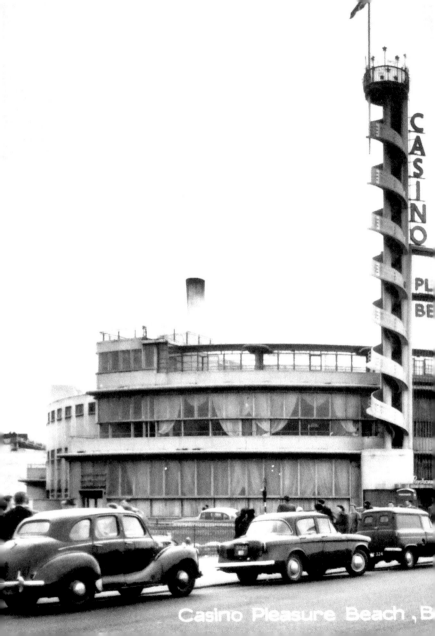

CASINO

PL
BE

Casino Pleasure Beach , B

44. THE CASINO, PLEASURE BEACH

The introduction of the modernist style of building throughout the Pleasure Beach was due to the engagement of architect Joseph Emberton in 1933 by Leonard Thompson, then the managing director of the Pleasure Beach. An earlier 'wedding cake'-style casino had been built in 1913. It was demolished in 1937 to make way for the modernist circular, reinforced-concrete building, which was built to Emberton's design. Despite the name of the first and the current buildings, gambling has never been part of the facilities at the casino.

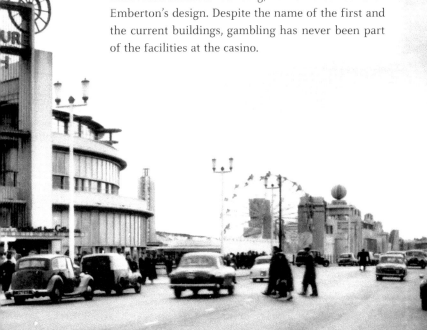

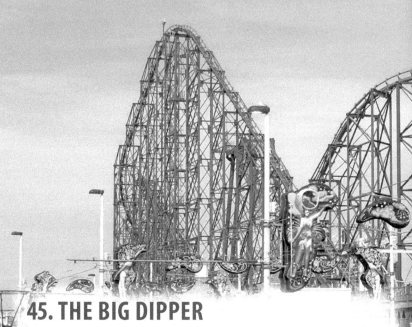

45. THE BIG DIPPER

The Big Dipper, which opened on 23 August 1923 on the beach at South Shore, is a classic wooden roller coaster. It was redesigned and extended in 1936. Between 1922 and 1926 the land in front of the Big Dipper was reclaimed and the New South Promenade to the southern boundary was constructed. The area between the Big Dipper and the Promenade was used as a boating lake for many years and is now the site of the originally named Pepsi Max 'Big One' (steel roller coaster), which opened on 28 May 1994.